In Memory of

Seymour
Lederberg

Professor of
Microbiology
Division of
Biology and Medicine
Brown University

BODY SYSTEMS

THE HUMAN BODY

BODY SYSTEMS

CELLS, TISSUES & ORGANS

DISEASES

EPIDEMICS & PANDEMICS

GENES & GENETICS

IMMUNOLOGY

MASON CREST

450 Parkway Drive, Suite D, Broomall, Pennsylvania 19008

(866) MCP-BOOK (toll-free)

James Shoals

First printing

9 8 7 6 5 4 3 2 1

ISBN (hardback) 978-1-4222-4192-9
ISBN (series) 978-1-4222-4191-2
ISBN (ebook) 978-1-4222-7611-2

Cataloging-in-Publication Data on file with the Library of Congress

Developed and Produced by National Highlights Inc.
Interior and cover design: Torque Advertising + Design
Production: Michelle Luke

THE SCIENCE OF THE HUMAN BODY

BODY SYSTEMS

JAMES SHOALS

MASON CREST

KEY ICONS TO LOOK FOR:

 Words to Understand: These words with their easy-to-understand definitions will increase the reader's understanding of the text while building vocabulary skills.

 Sidebars: This boxed material within the main text allows readers to build knowledge, gain insights, explore possibilities, and broaden their perspectives by weaving together additional information to provide realistic and holistic perspectives.

 Educational videos: Readers can view videos by scanning our QR codes, providing them with additional educational content to supplement the text. Examples include news coverage, moments in history, speeches, iconic sports moments, and much more!

 Text-Dependent Questions: These questions send the reader back to the text for more careful attention to the evidence presented there.

 Research Projects: Readers are pointed toward areas of further inquiry connected to each chapter. Suggestions are provided for projects that encourage deeper research and analysis.

QR CODES AND LINKS TO THIRD-PARTY CONTENT

CONTENTS

UNDERSTANDING BODY SYSTEMS

The human body is made up of several body systems, organs, numerous tissues, and billions of cells. Each system, organ, and tissue of the human body performs specialized functions.

Parts of the Human Body

- The head contains the brain.
- Eyes help us see.
- The nose helps us smell.
- The mouth helps us taste and eat.
- The chest is enclosed by the ribcage.
- The abdomen contains the digestive and reproductive organs.
- Fingers help us grasp.
- Hips support the lower limbs.
- Legs help us walk and run.
- Feet support the body's weight and allow movement.

 WORDS TO UNDERSTAND

secretion: biochemical released by the tissues and glands for the use of the organism or excretion.

tailbone: the final segment of human vertebrae.

vestigial: a leftover bit of something that used to be larger or more important.

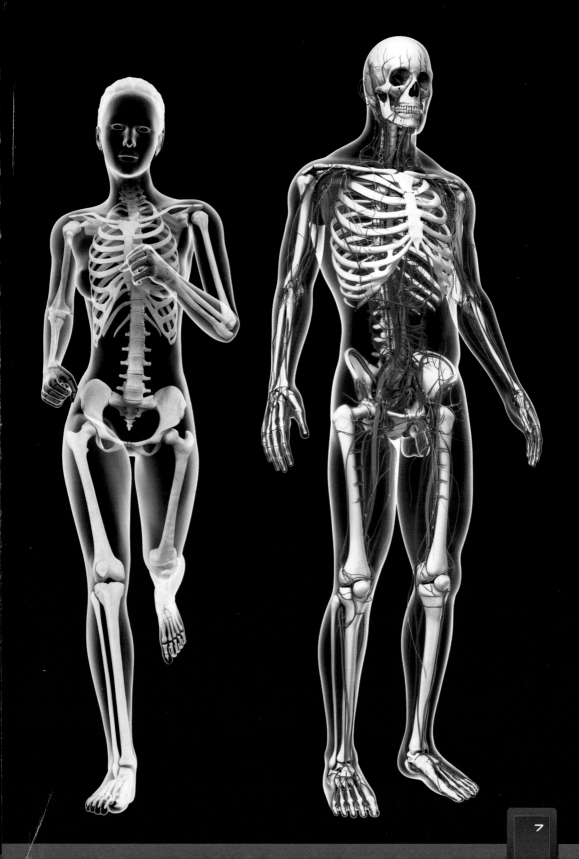

Organ Systems

Body systems are the most complex components of the human body. Each body system contains several organs that perform complex functions. Some systems, such as the nervous, skeletal, and muscular are found throughout the body, while others, such as the digestive, urinary, and endocrine systems are located in smaller areas.

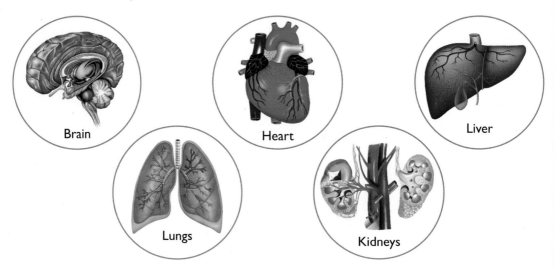

Brain

Heart

Liver

Lungs

Kidneys

Body Organs

Organs are an organization of several different kinds of tissues arranged together to perform special functions. Many organs such as the brain and the kidneys carry out multiple tasks.

- The brain controls and coordinates bodily activities and the senses.
- The heart pumps oxygenated blood into the body.
- The liver filters blood and cleans out toxic waste and acid in the blood.
- The stomach helps in the process of digestion.
- The kidneys filter blood and remove waste products and excess water from the body.
- The lungs pump oxygen and carbon dioxide in and out of our body.
- The small intestine absorbs food products.
- The large intestine absorbs water and excretes solid waste material.
- The skin helps to control body temperature and protects other organs from infection and injury.
- The pancreas produces various hormones.

Systems of the Human Body

- The skeletal system supports the human body and protects its internal organs.
- The muscular system allows the human body to move.
- The nervous system carries messages between the body and the brain.
- The circulatory system moves substances to and from the body cells.
- The digestive system digests and extracts energy and nutrients from food.
- The respiratory system controls the gaseous exchange in the body.
- The endocrine system controls the secretion of hormones from ductless glands.
- The immune system defends the body against diseases.
- The urinary system includes organs such as the kidneys and the large intestine. They work together to remove unwanted, undigested waste.
- The reproductive system includes organs that regulate the sexual functions of the body.

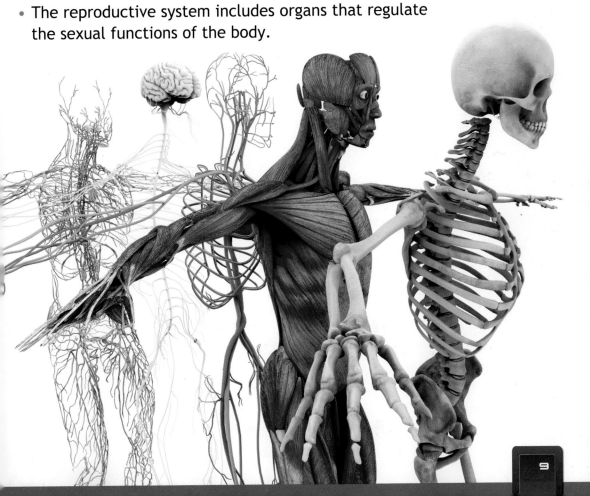

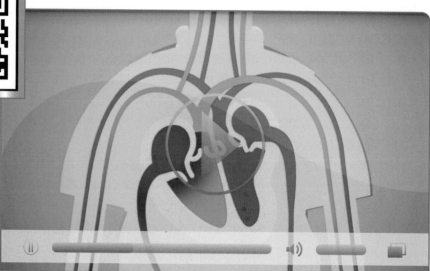

This video introduces you to the concept of body systems.

- Parts of the body that do not have any specific function are called vestigial; examples include the appendix, tailbone, and wisdom teeth.

- The liver is the largest and heaviest internal organ of the body. On average it weighs slightly over three pounds (about 1.5 kg).

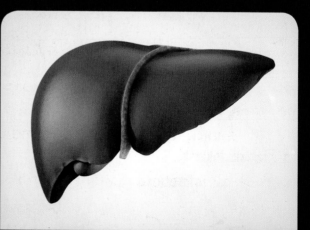

RESPIRATORY SYSTEM

Humans breathe in oxygen and breathe out carbon dioxide. The process of taking in air into the lungs is called inhalation, or inspiration, and the process of breathing it out is called exhalation, or expiration.

The whole process of the exchange of gases (oxygen and carbon dioxide) between the atmosphere and the cells of the body and vice versa is known as respiration. The system supplies oxygen to blood and in turn to every cell in the body. The process of respiration continues even at night while the body is at rest.

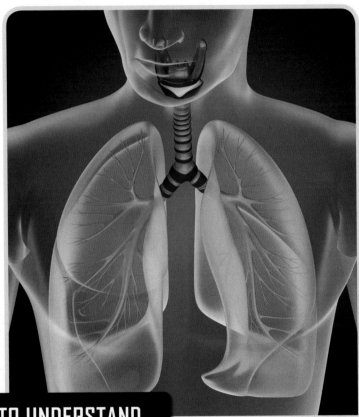

WORDS TO UNDERSTAND

chest cavity: the cavity, or hollow space, in the chest enclosed by ribs between the diaphragm and neck.

mucus: a thick fluid produced by some tissues that contains dead microorganisms.

pathogens: infectious microbes capable of causing disease.

Parts of the Respiratory System

The respiratory system is divided into two subgroups: the upper respiratory tract and lower respiratory tract. The upper respiratory tract includes the nose, nasal cavity, mouth, pharynx, and larynx, whereas the trachea and lungs make up the lower respiratory system.

Upper Respiratory Tract: Parts and Functions

Nose: As air enters through the nose, the mucous membrane warms and humidifies the air. Tiny hairs called cilia protect the nasal passage as well as the respiratory tract by filtering out dirt or dust and other foreign matter present in the breathed air. As air is inhaled, the cilia move back and forth to help in removing any harmful particles via nostrils.

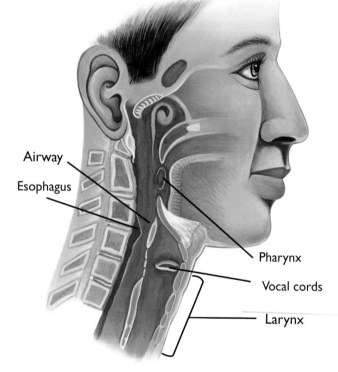

Airway

Esophagus

Pharynx

Vocal cords

Larynx

Pharynx: The pharynx lies at the back of the nose and mouth and acts as a carrier of air as well as food. Therefore, it is a part of the respiratory and digestive systems. At the end of the pharynx, the passage of air and food divides into the upper pharynx (air-only passage) and the lower pharynx, or esophagus.

Larynx: The larynx is known as the "voice box" because it's home to our vocals chords. It is the uppermost part of the air-only passage. It acts as a passageway for air between the pharynx and the trachea.

Lower Respiratory Tract: Parts and Functions

Trachea: The trachea, or windpipe, is the passage through which air enters or leaves the lungs. It extends downward from the base of the larynx and lies in between the neck and chest cavity. The trachea is strengthened with rings of cartilage so that air can flow easily before reaching the lungs. It is also lined with cilia to remove any foreign material from the airway and to further warm and moisten the air. At the bottom, the trachea divides into two bronchi tubes that join the lungs.

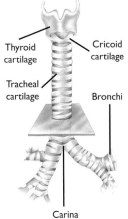

Thyroid cartilage

Cricoid cartilage

Tracheal cartilage

Bronchi

Carina

Lungs: Within the lungs, the bronchi divide into left and right bronchi, which further branch into bronchioles. Bronchioles are extremely thin and carry oxygen deeper into the lungs. At the end of bronchioles, tiny air sacs called alveoli transfer oxygen and absorb carbon dioxide from the blood.

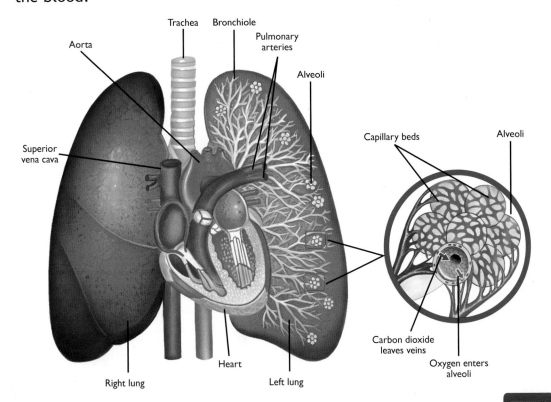

Trachea

Bronchiole

Pulmonary arteries

Aorta

Alveoli

Capillary beds

Alveoli

Superior vena cava

Alveoli

Carbon dioxide leaves veins

Oxygen enters alveoli

Heart

Right lung

Left lung

Breathing In, Breathing Out

While breathing in, the diaphragm contracts which pulls the rib cage up and out. The space within the chest increases which reduces the air pressure inside the lungs. Then air goes through bronchi and bronchioles and at last fills up the millions of alveolus. However, while breathing out, the diaphragm relaxes and the rib cage moves down. The space within the chest decreases which increases the air pressure inside the lungs.

The Respiration Process

The process of respiration begins with an individual inhaling air through the nose. The inhaled air reaches the nasal cavity, which acts as a filtering unit, trapping unwanted material with the help of nasal hair. The inhaled air then flows down the larynx, pharynx, past the trachea, which opens into the chest cavity. The trachea is divided into two bronchial tubes, which lead to the lungs. The bronchi are further divided into very small tubes called bronchioles. Each bronchiole divides into millions of tiny sacs called alveoli. Alveoli are the part of lungs where the essential gaseous exchange takes place. They are covered with numerous tiny

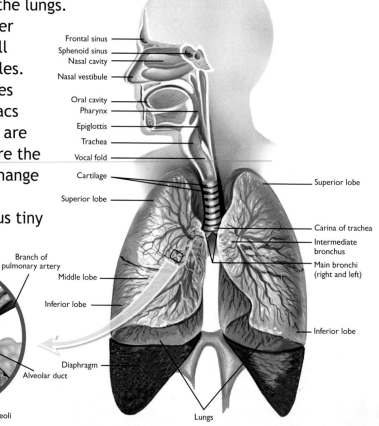

Frontal sinus
Sphenoid sinus
Nasal cavity
Nasal vestibule
Oral cavity
Pharynx
Epiglottis
Trachea
Vocal fold
Cartilage
Superior lobe
Superior lobe
Carina of trachea
Intermediate bronchus
Main bronchi (right and left)
Inferior lobe
Capillary beds
Arteriole
Branch of pulmonary artery
Pulmonary vein
Middle lobe
Inferior lobe
Respiratory bronchiole
Diaphragm
Alveolar duct
Connective tissue
Alveoli
Lungs

blood vessels known as capillaries. The walls of the alveoli and capillaries are very thin. This allows oxygen and carbon dioxide to pass through them, and travel in and out of the blood stream.

Maintaining a Healthy Respiratory System

People should not smoke and should stay away from people who do, because cigarette smoke is harmful for the lungs. Several respiratory diseases are caused by inhaling toxic substances that may enter the body through smoking or by attack of pathogens. The common cold, sinusitis, pneumonia, asthma, and tuberculosis (infection in respiratory tract) are a few of the respiratory diseases. People should always use a handkerchief or tissues when sneezing, coughing, or blowing their nose. Make sure to wear a mask if there is an outbreak of any respiratory disease or if the pollution levels in the air are too high. Exercising regularly and practicing deep breathing also helps in keeping the respiratory system healthy.

Larynx and Voice

The larynx plays an important role in producing sound. Sound is produced when the vocal cords close together and vibrate with the help of air that is expelled from the lungs.

Sneezing

When a person breathes in harmful particles, the mucous membrane feels irritated. The cilia present inside the nasal passage detects the objects and expels it from the nose in the form of a sneeze. Dirt, dust, pepper, pollen, or very cold air can irritate the inside of the nose.

SIDEBAR: DID YOU KNOW?

- We lose around 2 cups (around half a liter) of water a day through breathing.
- A person inhales and exhales about 22,000 times in a day.

DIGESTIVE SYSTEM

Taking in and absorbing the food is called digestion. The digestive system helps in digestion of food to provide energy to the body. Digestion is the chemical process of the breakdown of food into smaller particles so that the body can absorb them. The digestive system consists of a series of organs joined together that break down and absorb food. It is also responsible for gathering the bulk and fibrous waste to be excreted out of the body.

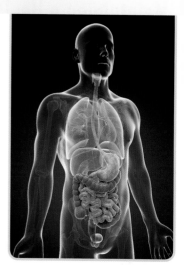

Parts of the Digestive System

Mouth: the first organ where food is broken down mechanically by chewing.

Esophagus: a tube that connects the mouth to the stomach.

Stomach: a hollow, muscular organ, that lies between the esophagus and the first part of the small intestine.

Intestines: the small and large intestines absorb the digested food, and feces are formed here.

Rectum: the temporary storage facility of feces.

Anus: the external opening of the rectum through which feces move out of the body.

 WORDS TO UNDERSTAND

alimentary: relating to nourishment.

fibrous: describes something with fiber, such as found in vegetables.

villi: microscopic, hairlike projections.

Alimentary Canal

The **alimentary** canal or digestive tract is the long, muscular digestive tube. It is more than 26 feet (about eight meters) in length. The digestive organs, such as the esophagus, stomach, small intestine, large intestine, and anus, are the parts of the alimentary canal.

The Digestion Process

The process of digestion starts in the mouth. The food is broken down by chewing and by the action of enzymes present in the saliva. After the food is swallowed, it is pushed into the esophagus that connects the throat to the stomach. The stomach muscles move in order to churn and mix the food with gastric juices. As most of the food needs further digestion, it travels into intestines.

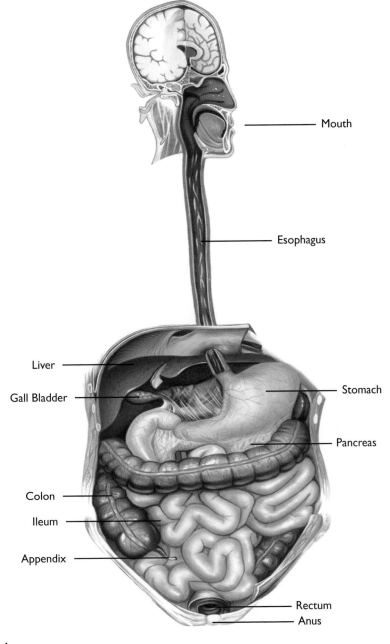

Mouth

Esophagus

Liver

Gall Bladder

Stomach

Pancreas

Colon

Ileum

Appendix

Rectum

Anus

Role of Small Intestines

The small intestine breaks down food into even smaller particles and turns it into a semiliquid mixture. Now all the nutrients from the semiliquid mixture are absorbed in with the help of villi on the inner walls of the small intestine. They absorb nutrients from food and pass those nutrients into the blood stream.

Role of Large Intestines

After absorption of nutrients, the remaining food matter is then passed into the five foot (1.5 meters) long large intestines, which is the last stop of the digestive tract. Here, the waste food passes through the colon where another attempt at extracting water and nutrients takes place. The remaining food waste is then removed from the body through the anus.

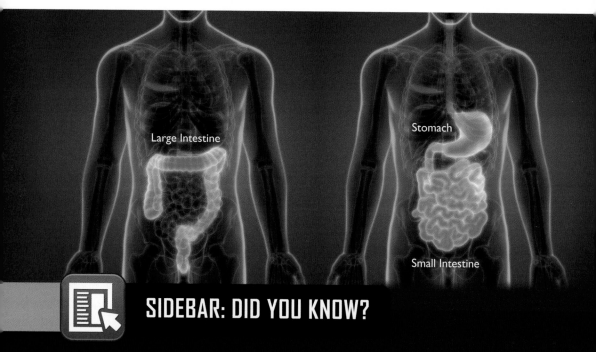

Large Intestine

Stomach

Small Intestine

SIDEBAR: DID YOU KNOW?

- **Peristalsis is a wavelike movement of muscles that pushes food through the digestive tract.**
- **Salivary glands produce saliva, which moistens the food and starts the process of digestion.**

WHY DIGESTION MATTERS

The body can't use foods for nourishment in their original form. The digestive system helps the body to break down food into small particles of nutrients so that they can be absorbed into the bloodstream and reach each cell in the body. The digestive system also helps in removing the excess food that the body does not need.

Chew Properly

Food should be chewed completely so that it can be easily swallowed. The mechanical action of chewing breaks down large particles of food into smaller particles. Well-chewed food mixes well with the saliva that helps in lubricating the food (even dry ones) to pass easily through the esophagus. When food is not chewed enough then incomplete digestion can take place.

Enzymes and Juices

The enzymes and juices secreted by the digestive system help in the digestion and absorption of food. Digestive juices are produced in the stomach,

WORDS TO UNDERSTAND

enzymes: substances produced by the body to cause a particular effect or reaction.

lubricating: describes something at makes movement smoother.

nourishment: getting all the required nutrients from the body.

intestines, and liver. These juices break down the food into smaller molecules that can be easily absorbed by the body. Bile is a digestive juice that dissolves fats and is produced by the liver. Enzymes are secreted in the mouth, stomach, and intestine. Enzymes such as pepsin, amylase, lipase break down carbohydrates, fats, and proteins.

Different Digestion for Different Foods

Digestion is a chemical process as it involves the action of enzymes and digestive juices. However, the chemical process of digestion differs for different types of food containing different types of nutrients.

Bread and Rice: Both bread and rice are carbohydrate-rich foods, which provide instant energy because their digestion begins as soon as they are consumed. Saliva secreted by the glands near the mouth start to break down the carbohydrates.

Meat and Eggs: Meat and eggs are protein-rich foods and their digestion begins in the stomach where stomach juices break down protein molecules. As the food passes through the small intestine, protein molecules are further broken down into amino acids, which are absorbed by the intestine walls.

Citrus Fruits and Broccoli: Citrus fruits and broccoli are rich sources of vitamins and fiber. Vitamins and fiber are extracted from the food in the stomach and later in the small intestine. Vitamins are absorbed whereas fiber helps in pushing the remaining food into the large intestine and later removed from the body as waste.

Healthy Digestive System

For a smooth digestion process, eat fresh food that's rich in fiber, such as bananas, spinach, and carrots. Wash your hands before and after eating to prevent the entry of germs into the body. Additionally, drink plenty of water for better absorption of ions and elimination of waste from the body.

 ## SIDEBAR: DID YOU KNOW?

- Food usually takes four to five hours to pass from one end of the small intestine to the other.

- The stomach secretes just under one gallon (1.5 liters) of gastric juices every day.

MUSCULAR SYSTEM

The muscular system is formed by the network of muscles found in the human body. The system provides movement to the body. The contraction and relaxation of muscle fibers help in movement, maintaining body posture, and circulating blood throughout the body. The nervous system controls and operates the movements of the muscular system. However, muscles of the heart move independently. The muscular system is also responsible for the functioning of important organs in the body such as the heart and lungs.

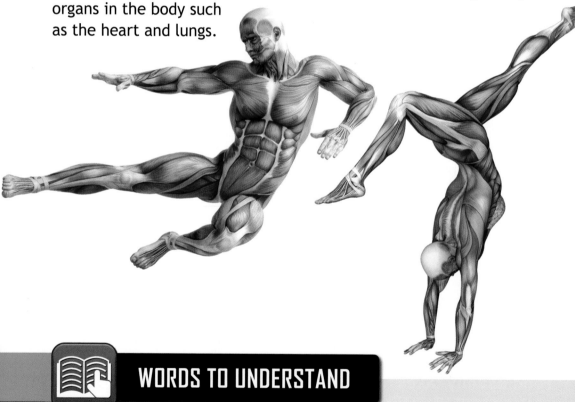

WORDS TO UNDERSTAND

contraction: tightening.
cardiac: relating to the heart.
involuntary: something that can't be controlled or is against the will.

Voluntary and Involuntary Muscles

There are two basic types of muscles in the body: voluntary and involuntary. Involuntary muscles work on their own without receiving signals from the brain. Examples include the heart beating, the eyes blinking, and so on. On the other hand, voluntary muscles work when the brain tells them to, such as when you are clapping, jumping, walking, etc.

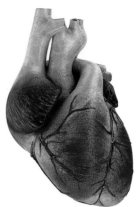

Types of Muscles

There are three types of muscles in the body: skeletal, cardiac, and smooth. Skeletal muscles are attached to the skeleton. They are voluntary muscles and are responsible for the movement of the body. They provide power and strength to the body. Smooth muscles, on the other hand, are involuntary muscles and are found in the digestive system, blood vessels, bladder, airways, and uterus.

Cardiac muscles are found only in the heart. They are involuntary muscles that help the heart to pump blood throughout the body nonstop.

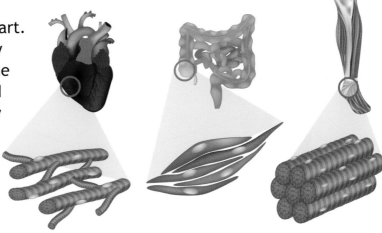

Cardiac Muscle   Smooth Muscle   Skeletal Muscle

Muscle Structure

Muscles are made of subunits known as fascicles. Fascicles have bundle-like structure. They contain muscle fibers. Muscle fibers are made of several myofibrils. Myofibrils are thin, cylindrical rods made of several proteins, such as actin and myosin. The myofibrils contain protein filaments called thick and thin myofilaments.

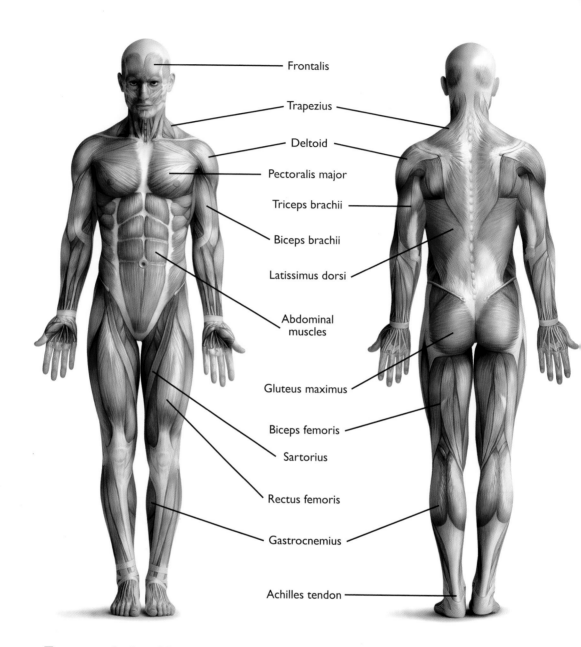

Frontalis

Trapezius

Deltoid

Pectoralis major

Triceps brachii

Biceps brachii

Latissimus dorsi

Abdominal muscles

Gluteus maximus

Biceps femoris

Sartorius

Rectus femoris

Gastrocnemius

Achilles tendon

Parts of the Muscular System

The frontalis covers the forehead. The temporalis covers the ear.
The orbicularis covers eyes and lips. The masseter covers the jaw.
The sternocleidomastoid covers the neck. The pectoralis major covers
the upper part of the chest. The rectus abdominis covers the abdomen.
The trapezius covers from the neck to the middle of the back.

Many Muscles

The human body's muscular system is composed of more than 640 active muscles. These muscles act in groups. But not all of these muscles have particular names. These muscles range in size from the tiny stapedius muscle in the middle ear to the large quadriceps in the thighs.

The latissimus dorsi covers the lower back. The deltoid covers the shoulders. The biceps brachii covers the front of the upper arm. The triceps brachii covers the rear of the upper arm. The gluteus maximus covers the hip. The quadriceps covers the front of the thigh. The hamstrings cover the back of the thigh. The gastrocnemius is also known as calf muscles.

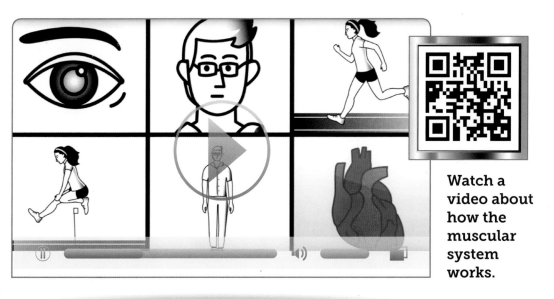

Watch a video about how the muscular system works.

 SIDEBAR: DID YOU KNOW?

- Muscles always act and work in pairs to produce movements in the body.
- The busiest muscles in the body are the eye muscles. They may move more than 100,000 times a day.

MUSCLES AND MOVEMENT

Muscles help human beings perform small activities such as smile, blink, clap, breathe, speak, etc., by consuming energy. They are made up of thousands of long, thin fibers called muscle fibers. There are different types of muscle movements as well as a proper process of working of muscles.

How Do Muscles Work?

A muscle fiber is composed of cells that have a contractile unit called the sarcomere. The sarcomere is made up of the proteins actin and myosin. The myosin is a thick myofilament whereas actin is a thin myofilament. These myofilaments slide over each other using the stored energy in the muscles and cause contraction. During contraction, the muscle cells

 WORDS TO UNDERSTAND

contractile: describes something that is capable of contraction.

reflexive action: an action that occurs automatically in response to a signal.

steroids: short for "anabolic steroids," these are synthetic hormones that affect the muscles.

become shorter and fatter. Shorter and fatter muscle cells in the muscles means greater contraction power of the muscles. However, the opposite happens during relaxation of muscles. The actin and myosin filaments move apart and the muscle stretches.

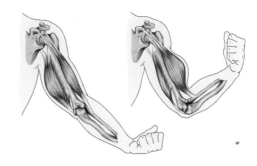

What is Shivering?

Shivering is an action in which a person's body begins to tremble in an involuntary manner, especially when the body temperature falls below normal. It is a reflexive action of the body, which keeps a person safe and healthy. Reflexive actions are usually controlled by the nervous system, which includes the brain, spinal cord, and hundreds of nerves. These nerves sense the low temperature of the body and send signals to the brain and spinal cord, which send signals to muscles to tighten and loosen at a fast pace. It causes shivering which generates heat in the body. It also makes a person to look for ways to warm the body.

What are Goosebumps?

Goosebumps appear on the skin when we're cold or scared. Because skin is covered with hair, when small muscles beneath the skin contract, they pull the hair. This makes the hair stand up. The bumps are called *goosebumps* because they look like the skin of a goose.

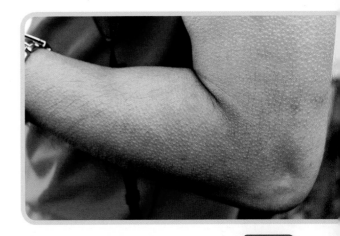

Healthy Muscular System

For a healthy muscular system, exercise is very important. Regular exercise makes the muscles strong and maintains body temperature. A person should eat lots of fruits and vegetables as part of a balanced diet. Foods rich in protein, such as milk, yogurt, and fish, help make the muscles stronger. Never consume steroids without medical supervision. Contrary to what advertising might suggest, steroids can damage muscles instead of making them strong.

SIDEBAR: DID YOU KNOW?

- **The diaphragm is a muscle wall. It separates the chest from the abdomen.**

- **Muscles make up about 40 percent of your total body weight.**

URINARY SYSTEM

The urinary system is another vital system of the human body that works to remove waste products out of the body. Several organs of the urinary system work in coordination to keep the body clean. The urinary system filters out excess fluids and wastes, like urea, from the blood in the form of urine.

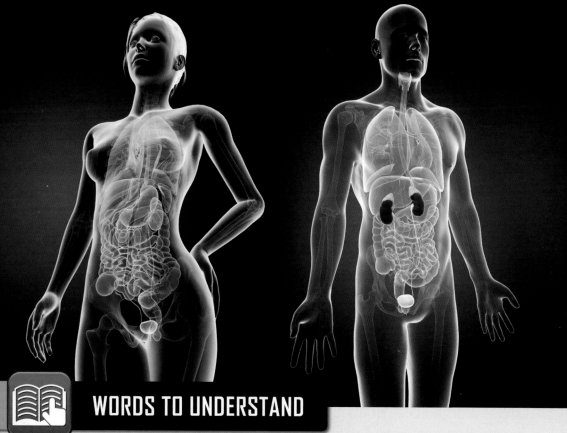

WORDS TO UNDERSTAND

dehydration: a medical condition in which the body suffers from lack of water.
flexible: the ability to bend or move with flow.
pigment: an element that is responsible for providing color.
sphincter: a ring of muscle that can open and close.
urea: a compound that is created by the process of breaking down food.

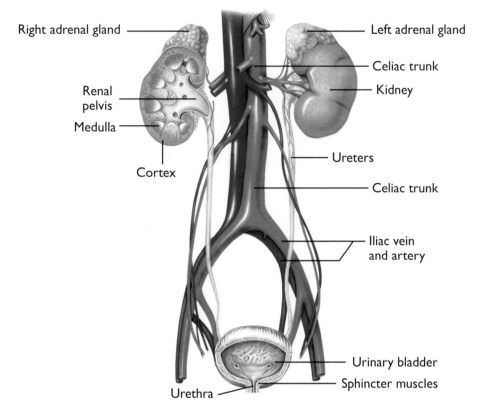

Right adrenal gland

Left adrenal gland

Celiac trunk

Renal pelvis

Kidney

Medulla

Cortex

Ureters

Celiac trunk

Iliac vein and artery

Urinary bladder

Sphincter muscles

Urethra

Parts and Functions

Kidneys: They are the main organs of the urinary system. Kidneys are about ten centimeters long, and are bean-shaped organs.

Ureters: They are long muscular tubes that transport urine from the kidneys to the urinary bladder. Ureters are usually 10 to 12 inches (25 to 30 cm) long in an adult.

Urinary Bladder: The urinary bladder is a large and hollow triangular-shaped organ that holds urine. It can hold around two cups (around half a liter) of urine for about two to five hours. The walls of the bladder contract to let the urine pass out of the body through another tube, the urethra.

Urethra: The urethra connects the urinary bladder to the outside of the body. It is longer in males—about 7.8 inches (20 cm).

Sphincter muscles: two sphincter muscles help keep urine from leaking.

What is Urine?

Urine contains water in large quantities along with ammonia, urea, urochrome, and creatinine. Urea is the chief component of urine that is released from the breakdown of proteins. Foods such as meat, chicken, and some vegetables contain these proteins. Urochrome is a  pigment that gives urine its yellow color. Creatinine, on the other hand, is a waste product that is released as a regular breakdown of muscle byproducts of bile from the liver.

Color Indicator

Urine is made up of water and the waste materials that are filtered out of the blood. If people drink enough water, it appears lighter in color. However, if people play and sweat a lot, and do not drink water or juices, then the urine has more waste material and less water and would appear darker.

How Does It Work?

The kidneys have more than one million filtering units called nephrons. The nephrons are made up of two parts: the glomerulus and the Bowman's capsule. Glomerulus is a network of capillaries and blood vessels, which bring impure blood to the kidneys, while the Bowman's capsule is a saclike, double-layered structure at the top. The kidneys absorb the maximum amount of water and ions. The remaining large protein molecules and salts are stored in the bladder.

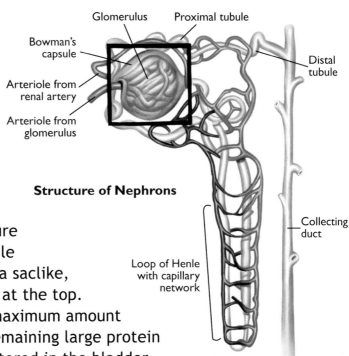

Glomerulus   Proximal tubule

Bowman's capsule

Arteriole from renal artery

Arteriole from glomerulus

Distal tubule

Structure of Nephrons

Loop of Henle with capillary network

Collecting duct

When the bladder is filled with salts and other substances, it contracts to release the waste out of the body.

Healthy Urinary System

For a healthy urinary system, people should drink plenty of fluids. Drinking water and fluids in optimum amount reduces the risk of kidney stones and urinary tract infections. They are two of the most common ailments of the urinary system. Make sure to drink plenty of water while out in the sun or exercising. Reduce the intake of salt in food to help retain water in the body. If possible, avoid drinking carbonated drinks and coffee. Go to the bathroom when you need to go, as holding urine for too long puts pressure on the bladder and is not good for the urinary tract.

Blood Purifier

Another function of the urinary system is to filter out excess fluid and other substances from the body. The kidneys filter all the blood in the body 20 or more times every day. The kidneys also produce a hormone that regulates the production of red blood cells, and they play a role in maintaining normal blood pressure.

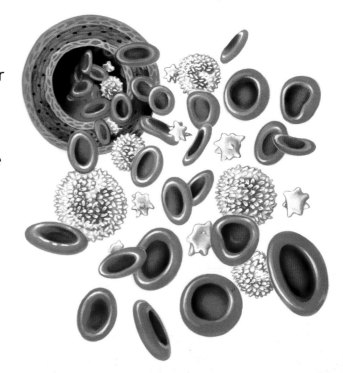

Aging and Urinary System

With age, the number and size of nephrons decreases. As a result, waste materials and excess fluids are not completely filtered out of the body. The kidneys also shrink in size because of the decline in the number of nephrons. As kidneys become smaller, less blood flows through them. Kidneys also reduce their ability to maintain a balance of salts and other chemicals, posing a greater risk of dehydration. The urinary bladder becomes less flexible and holds less urine. The sphincter muscles also reduce their ability to close tightly to prevent any leakage.

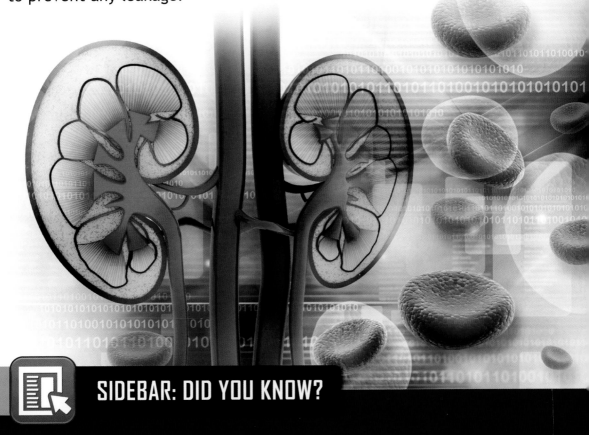

SIDEBAR: DID YOU KNOW?

- Each kidney has about one million nephrons.
- The first successful kidney transplant was performed in 1954.

ENDOCRINE SYSTEM

The endocrine system is made up of several ductless glands that secrete chemical compounds known as hormones. The glands release hormones into the bloodstream, where they are transported to tissues and organs throughout your body. There are different types of hormones and each hormone performs a separate function.

What are Hormones?

The word *hormone* means to "spur on," which aptly describes the prime function of hormones. Hormones carry messages to cells. They cause changes in the body to begin and then regulate those changes. There are more than 30 hormones busily initiating and regulating changes such as hunger, sleep, growth, and so on.

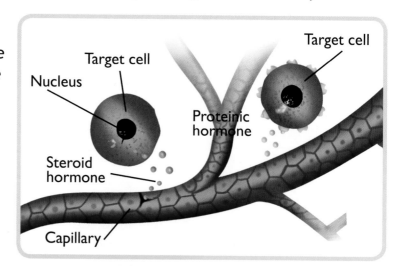

 WORDS TO UNDERSTAND

gland: an organ which releases chemical substances.

glucagon: a hormone that increases low blood sugar level.

insulin: a substance that controls blood sugar level in blood.

metabolism: the process by which energy from nutrients and minerals is acquired by the body.

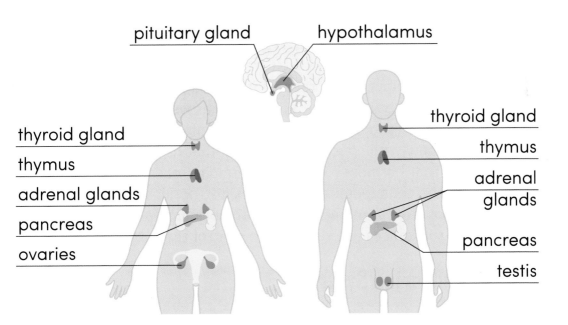

pituitary gland　　　　hypothalamus

thyroid gland

thyroid gland

thymus

thymus

adrenal glands

adrenal glands

pancreas

pancreas

ovaries

testis

Parts of the Endocrine System

The endocrine system is made up of glands located around the body.

- **Pituitary gland** regulates and controls growth and other glands. It is also called "master gland".
- **Thyroid gland** regulate the rate of growth and metabolism.
- **Parathyroid gland** regulates calcium balance in the body.
- **Thymus** is necessary for development of the immune system.
- **Pancreas** produces two important hormones: insulin and glucagon. It is responsible for controlling blood sugar levels.
- **Adrenal glands** regulate salt and water content in the body, and helps in dealing with stress.
- **Gonads** produce sex hormones in both males and females.

Functions of Endocrine System

Hormones produced by the endocrine glands help in regulation of growth, development, metabolism, moods, behavior, and feelings in human beings. The system controls and maintains the body's energy levels. It also helps in the absorption of nutrients. It encourages the body to respond to its surroundings, stress, anxiety, and injury.

How the Endocrine System Works

When a gland secretes a hormone, it travels through the bloodstream to the cell that is supposed to receive its message. Those particular cells are called target cells. The target cells as well as the hormones have their own receptors. Therefore, the specific hormone will communicate only with specific target cells that have the same receptors for that hormone. When the hormone reaches its target cells, it binds with the cells receptors and gives instructions to the cells. When the amount of hormones reaches an optimum level, certain hormones or substances are secreted to control the further secretion.

Healthy Endocrine System

Eat a diet rich in proteins, omega, vitamins, minerals, and calcium for a healthy endocrine system. Include garlic as it improves immunity and helps in regulating blood sugar levels. Eat slowly so that the body can digest food easily and efficiently. Exercising regularly and consuming plenty of fluids are good for the system. If the endocrine system does not work efficiently, a person may suffer from fatigue, weight gain or weight loss, hair loss, sleep disorders, or improper growth and development.

SIDEBAR: DID YOU KNOW?

- The endocrine system secretes 30 different types of hormones.
- A treatment called hormone replacement therapy (HRT) can sometimes help ease symptoms of aging in older women.

SKELETAL SYSTEM

The skeletal system provides shape, structure, and support to the body. It is made up of bones and cartilage that surround and protect the vital organs of the body like the brain, heart, and lungs. The skeleton continues to change its composition over a lifespan. Babies are born with about 300 bones, but some bones fuse together as they grow. Adults end up with 206 bones. The skeletal system is divided into two parts: the axial skeleton and the appendicular system.

Axial Skeleton

The axial skeleton comprises of 80 bones of the upper body and includes the skull, vertebrae of the backbone, ribs, and breastbone. These bones form the vertical axis of the body. The skull is the bony structure of the head, which encloses the brain and supports the jaws. The cranium is a part of the skull that supports the brain. The mandibles and maxillae are the jawbones. The vertebral column is the backbone consisting of 33 small bones known as vertebrae. The rib cage has 12 pairs of rib bones.

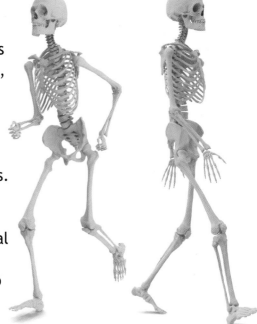

 WORDS TO UNDERSTAND

appendicular: relating to an appendage; here, arms and legs.
axial: relating to an axis.
cartilage: a flexible tissue that connects bones.
girdles: here, sets of bones to which the arms and legs are attached.

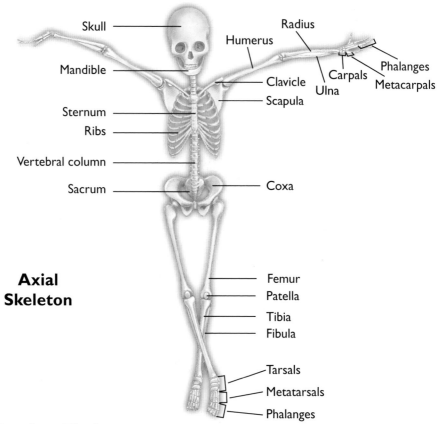

Skull

Radius

Humerus

Mandible

Phalanges

Clavicle

Carpals

Ulna

Metacarpals

Scapula

Sternum

Ribs

Vertebral column

Sacrum

Coxa

**Axial
Skeleton**

Femur

Patella

Tibia

Fibula

Tarsals

Metatarsals

Phalanges

Appendicular Skeleton

The appendicular skeleton consists of the bones of the limbs, shoulders, and their attachments, which are called girdles. There are 126 bones in the appendicular skeleton. The upper limbs are attached to the shoulder or pectoral girdle and the lower limbs are attached to the pelvic or hip girdle.

Pectoral Girdle and Pelvic Girdle

The pectoral girdle has two shoulder blades and two collarbones, which allow some movement to the body. On the other hand, the pelvic girdle has two large hipbones and each hipbone consists of three fused bones called the ilium, ischium, and pubis. The ilium forms the upper part of the pelvis, the ischium forms the lower part, and the pubis forms the central part. However, unlike the axial system, the appendicular system is not fused, which allows a great deal of motion.

Functions of the Skeletal System

Without skeletal system's support, the body would collapse. It provides protection to delicate organs of the body—for instance, the ribcage protects the heart and lungs, and vertebrae protect the spinal cord. Along with the muscles it helps in the movement of the body. The system also provides stability in the movements. Bones also store minerals such as calcium and phosphorus, which are released when the body needs them.

Healthy Skeletal System

Exercises such as walking, jogging, and running are good to keep the skeletal system healthy. Cycling, playing soccer, basketball, and so on, are also good for bones. However, make sure to wear protective gear such as helmets and knee guards to keep the skeletal system safe. Eat foods rich in calcium such as dairy products and increase your intake of vitamin D because it helps in absorbing calcium.

SIDEBAR: DID YOU KNOW?

- **The longest bone of the skeletal system is the thighbone, or femur.**
- **The "stirrup" in the ear is the smallest bone.**

MUSCULOSKELETAL SYSTEM

The muscles and skeleton together make up the musculoskeletal system, which is made up of bones, joints, muscles, cartilage, tendons, and ligaments. Apart from supporting the weight of the body, bones work along with muscles to allow flexible, controlled, and precise movements. To perform different movements, different bones are connected by different joints. The primary function of the musculoskeletal system is to provide support to the body, allow motion, and protect delicate organs.

What Supports the Skeletal Framework?

The skeletal system is made of individual or joined bones. The bones are classified as long, short, flat, and irregular bones. Ligaments, tendons, muscles, and cartilage, support the bones of the skeletal system.

 WORDS TO UNDERSTAND

joints: here, the points at which two bones are connected.
ligaments: short, tough bands of tissue that surround joints.
tendons: tissue that attaches muscles and bones.

Bones and Joints

Bones are strong connective tissues that form the skeletal system. The central cavity of the bone contains the bone marrow, which produces blood cells and platelets. Joints are located at the place where two bones meet. They help the bones to move and protect them from damaging each other.

Tendons

Tendons are tough bands of connective tissue that attach muscles to bones. They, along with muscles, help the body move. They are a little elastic and help a person to walk, run, grab and hold objects, etc. Therefore, without tendons the body would not be able to move the way it does. Tendons grow into the bones and form a tough connection, which creates a strong permanent bond.

Ligaments

Ligaments are connective tissues, which hold bones together at joints. They stabilize joints so that the bones can move in proper alignment. Ligaments allow certain joints to move, control their movements, and range of motion. They usually stretch when under stress and come back to their normal position when the stress is removed. However, ligaments lose their original shape and position if stretched for extended period. This is the reason dislocated joints need to be set as soon as possible.

Cartilage

Cartilage is a type of stiff and flexible connective tissue found in many areas of the body. It provides a cushioning effect to joints. There are three types of main cartilage in the body such as hyaline cartilage, elastic cartilage, and fibrocartilage. It prevents bones from rubbing against each other. Cartilage can be found in joints, the rib cage, ears, nose, throat, and between intervertebral disks in the spinal cord.

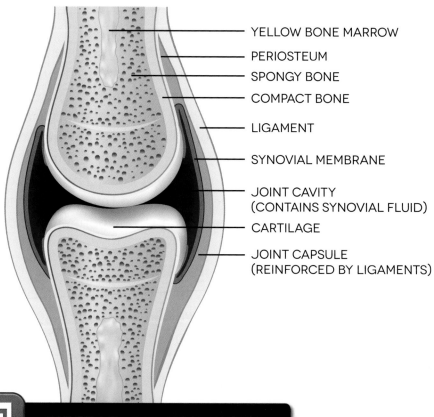

YELLOW BONE MARROW

PERIOSTEUM

SPONGY BONE

COMPACT BONE

LIGAMENT

SYNOVIAL MEMBRANE

JOINT CAVITY
(CONTAINS SYNOVIAL FLUID)

CARTILAGE

JOINT CAPSULE
(REINFORCED BY LIGAMENTS)

 SIDEBAR: DID YOU KNOW?

- The human body has 360 joints.
- Bones in women tend to be smaller and less dense than in men, even when their bodies are of similar size.

REPRODUCTIVE SYSTEM

Reproduction is the biological process of the formation of a new life. All living things reproduce. The reproductive system is different in males and females. It requires two kinds of sex cells: the sperm from the male and the egg, or ovum, from the female. The process of reproduction starts when the sperm fertilizes the egg.

Parts of the Male Reproductive System

- **Testes** produces and stores millions of sperm cells.
- **Scrotum** is the external pouch that contains the testis.
- **Vas deferens** is the duct that transports sperm containing the fluid called semen.
- **Penis** is the external reproductive organ.

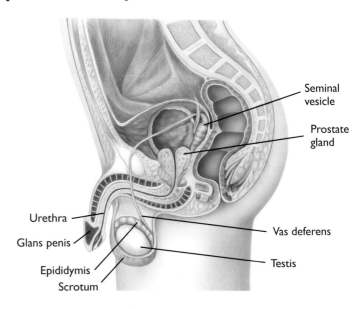

Seminal vesicle

Prostate gland

Urethra

Glans penis

Vas deferens

Epididymis

Testis

Scrotum

WORDS TO UNDERSTAND

ovum: a female reproductive cell.

fertilization: here, the combination of male and female cells that leads to the formation of a new organism.

fetus: the unborn offspring of a mammal.

zygote: a fertilized ovum.

Parts of the Female Reproductive System

- **Ovaries** are small, paired organs, located in the pelvis, one on each side of the uterus.
- **Uterus** is located in the lower abdomen between the bladder and the rectum. It supports the fetus during pregnancy. It is also called a womb.
- **Placenta** is a flat organ inside the uterus that nourishes the **fetus** as it grows.
- **Fallopian tubes** join the ovary and the uterus. They have small hair (cilia) to help the egg cell travel from the ovaries to uterus.
- **Birth canal** is the passage from the womb to the cervix.

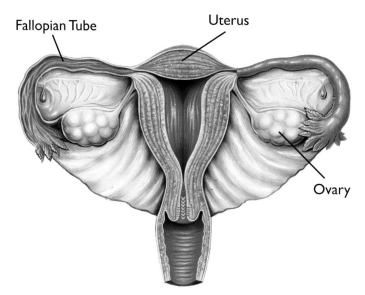

Fallopian Tube

Uterus

Ovary

How Do They Work?

Gonads are paired organs that produce sex hormones in both males and females during puberty. In males, the gonads are testes and in females the gonads are ovaries. The testes produce the male hormone testosterone while the ovaries produce the female hormones estrogen and progesterone. During sexual intercourse, the testes release sperm, which fertilize the ovum produced by ovaries. The fertilization results in the formation of a cell called a zygote. The zygote attaches itself to the wall of the uterus in the female's body and develops into an embryo. The embryo grows, and after eight weeks it is called a fetus.

Growth of a Fetus

The fetus develops and grows inside the uterus. The embryonic layers and organs are formed during the first three weeks of pregnancy. After four months, the bony part of the skeleton is formed and the fetus grows in size. After seven months, the circulatory and respiratory systems mature, and by the end of the ninth month, the baby is ready for birth.

SIDEBAR: DID YOU KNOW?

- The ovum is the largest cell in the human body while the sperm is the smallest.

- Under certain conditions, sperm can live as long as five days. The average lifespan is closer to three.

NERVOUS SYSTEM

The nervous system is the control and communication center of the body. It manages everything we do: think, react, learn or remember, and even sleep. It is made up of many nerve cells. Each nerve cell is made up of two parts: a neuron and glial cell. Neurons transmit messages from the organs to the brain and vice versa, while glial cells cover and protect the neurons.

Parts of the Nervous System

The nervous system is divided into two parts—central nervous system and the peripheral nervous system. These two parts of the nervous system work together for the body to communicate its needs.

Central Nervous System

The central nervous system (CNS) is made of the brain and spinal cord. The skull protects the brain whereas the spinal cord is protected by the vertebral column. These bones protect the central nervous system and act as a shield in case of injury.

WORDS TO UNDERSTAND

autonomic: involuntary.
glial: refers to the connective tissue of the nervous system.
meninges: membranes that enclose the spinal cord.
neuron: a specialized nerve cell that carries impulses.
peripheral: describes something on the edge or off to the side.
somatic: relating to the body (as opposed to the mind).

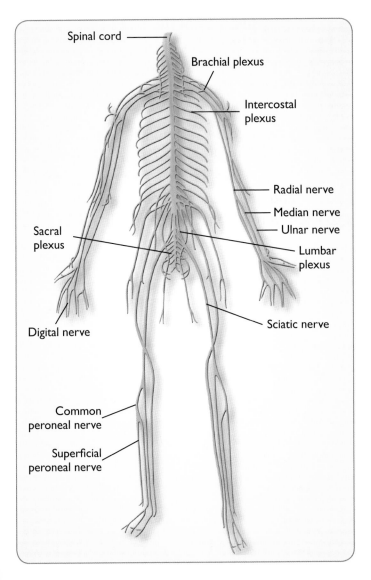

Spinal cord

Brachial plexus

Intercostal plexus

Radial nerve

Median nerve

Ulnar nerve

Lumbar plexus

Sacral plexus

Sciatic nerve

Digital nerve

Common peroneal nerve

Superficial peroneal nerve

Peripheral Nervous System

The peripheral nervous system (PNS) comprises of all the nerves and nerve cells that lie outside the central nervous system. It transmits information from the brain and spinal cord to the rest of the body and from the rest of the body to the brain and the spinal cord. The system has 12 pairs of cranial nerves, which emerge out the of the brain and are related to the head and neck. In addition, there are 31 pairs of spinal nerves that branch out from the spinal cord, carrying information throughout the body. However, unlike the central nervous system there is no bony protection for the peripheral nervous system.

Voluntary Actions

The peripheral nervous system allows a person to perform voluntary and involuntary actions. This is why it is divided into two parts, which are called the somatic nervous system and autonomic nervous system. The somatic nervous system is made up of neurons that carry

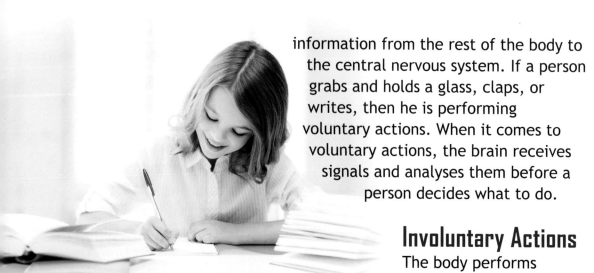

information from the rest of the body to the central nervous system. If a person grabs and holds a glass, claps, or writes, then he is performing voluntary actions. When it comes to voluntary actions, the brain receives signals and analyses them before a person decides what to do.

Involuntary Actions

The body performs actions such as beating of the heart and digestion of food involuntarily. These involuntary actions are controlled by the autonomic nervous system. The autonomic nervous system is made up of motor neurons, or autonomic neurons. These motor neurons are responsible for regulating heartbeat, the process of digestion, and the release of hormones from certain glands.

Fight or Flight

The autonomic nervous system has two parts: sympathetic and parasympathetic nervous systems. The sympathetic nervous system prepares the body to deal with sudden stressful situations. It is the body's alarm for danger and stress. The system raises blood pressure, heart rate, as well as breathing rate to enable the body to take quick action in emergencies. It also causes the adrenal glands to secrete the adrenaline hormone, which provides extra power to muscles. This response is called fight or flight response.

Relax and Digest

The parasympathetic nervous system is sometimes called the "rest and digest" system. It helps in conserving and restoring the body's energy. The system also works in making digestion a smooth process so that the body can extract maximum amounts of nutrients from food. It keeps blood pressure, heart rate, and breathing at normal rate or even at low levels when at rest.

Functions of the Nervous System

The sensory neurons gather information from the external environment and then assess all the collected information. Then the system generates a motor response with the help of motor neurons that send nerve impulses to the relevant parts of the body.

Sending and Receiving Signals

A neuron starts functioning when a stimulus (change of temperature, sense of touch, etc.) is generated. It has three parts: dendrite, cell body, and axon, which help in transferring signals also known as impulses. Several neurons combine to form bundles of nerve fibers. The nerve fibers form long pathways from the organ to the brain. The impulse travels through these nerve pathways. The nerve cells are covered by special glial cells called Schwann cells. These cells help in faster transmission of signals. Once the signal reaches the brain, a reaction occurs. The nerves that transmit the signal to the brain are called sensory nerves while the nerves that take the signal back to the organ are called motor nerves.

Healthy Nervous System

For a healthy nervous system, people should eat a nutritious diet rich in vitamin B^{12} and low in fats. Performing activities such as exercising and playing sports keep the mind as well the body healthy. It's best to avoid smoking and drinking alcohol, and try to avoid tension and stress.

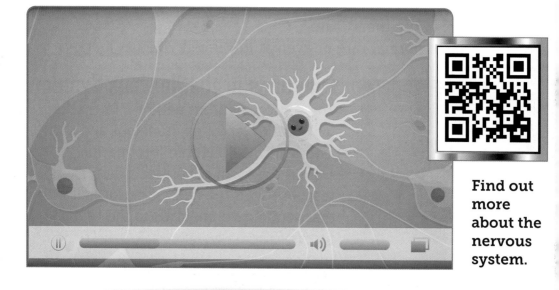

Find out more about the nervous system.

SIDEBAR: DID YOU KNOW?

- The nervous system can transmit messages to the brain at the speed of 180 miles per hour!
- The central nervous system is protected by a three-layered tissue known as meninges. There are three layers: dura mater, arachnoid mater, and pia mater.

CIRCULATORY SYSTEM

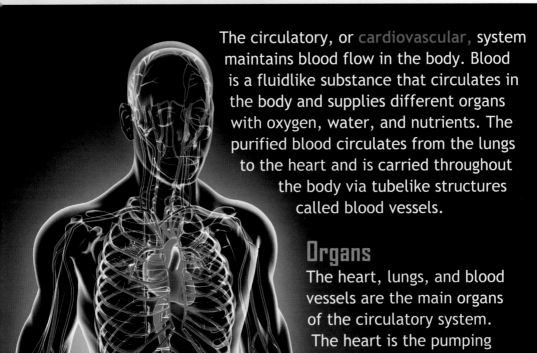

The circulatory, or cardiovascular, system maintains blood flow in the body. Blood is a fluidlike substance that circulates in the body and supplies different organs with oxygen, water, and nutrients. The purified blood circulates from the lungs to the heart and is carried throughout the body via tubelike structures called blood vessels.

Organs

The heart, lungs, and blood vessels are the main organs of the circulatory system. The heart is the pumping organ of the body. It has four chambers, the two upper chambers are called atria and the two lower chambers are called ventricles.

WORDS TO UNDERSTAND

cardiovascular: relating to the heart and blood vessels.
coronary: describes things occurring in the heart, such as coronary disease, coronary artery, and so on.
pulmonary: relating to the lungs and breathing.

After reaching the heart, blood travels to the lungs for purification. Now the purified blood comes back to the heart and is supplied to all other parts of the body via a network of blood vessels. Blood vessels play a crucial role in blood circulation. They are tubelike canals that circulate blood to and from all parts of the body. Veins, arteries, and capillaries are three types of blood vessels.

Superior vena cava

Aorta

Pulmonary Veins

Pulmonary arteries

Inferior vena cava

Descending aorta

Femoral vein

Femoral artery

Arteries

Arteries carry oxygenated blood away from the heart to cells, tissues, and organs. The heart pumps out blood from one main artery called aorta. The aorta then divides smaller arteries and branches further into smaller arteries known as arterioles. They are strong as well as flexible because they sustain the powerful blood flow from the heart. When the heart is at rest, arteries contract with enough force to push blood along. An artery is made up of three layers: an outer layer of tissue, a muscular middle layer, and an inner layer of special (epithelial) cells.

Capillaries

The tiniest blood vessels are capillaries, which connect arteries and veins. They are responsible for transferring oxygen, nutrients, and waste products to and from blood.

Veins

Veins are blood vessels that carry deoxygenated and impure blood to the heart. They receive blood from capillaries when the exchange of oxygen and waste products has taken place. Veins branch into venules and supply blood at lower pressure as compared to arteries. They are also not as strong as arteries and allow blood to flow in one direction. There are valves inside veins that prevent impure blood from flowing backwards.

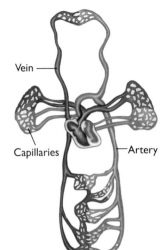

Blood Pressure

Blood circulates all over the body through a network of blood vessels with great force. The heart provides this force and pressure when the ventricles contract and compel blood out of the heart and into the arteries. However, the pressure drops when the ventricles relax to refill with blood. Pressure of blood varies throughout the body. Blood pressure varies and depends upon the activities a person performs. High blood pressure is a serious medical condition in which a person suffers from high blood pressure even when at rest.

How It Works

The heart pumps purified blood brought in from the lungs, to various parts of the body through arteries and capillaries. Veins collect impure blood from various organs and carry it to the heart for purification. The heart pumps this blood into the pulmonary artery, which carries it to the lungs. The lungs enrich blood with oxygen and then the oxygen-rich blood enters the heart through the pulmonary veins. The heart transfers this blood to arteries, which circulate it to every cell via capillaries. Capillaries extract deoxygenated blood from body cells and transfer it to the veins. The circulatory system is divided into three systems: the pulmonary system, coronary system and systemic system.

Pulmonary Circulation

Pulmonary circulation is the circulation of blood between the heart and lungs. In this circulation, veins bring back oxygen-less blood to the heart where it enters the right atrium. The right atrium then pushes the blood towards the right ventricle from where the blood is carried to the lungs via the pulmonary artery. Inside the lungs, purification of blood takes place and the oxygen-rich blood returns back to the heart via pulmonary veins. The blood enters the heart through the left atrium and then it passes to the left ventricle from where it leaves the heart and begins its journey throughout the body.

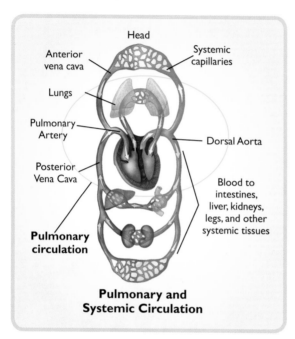

Labels: Head, Anterior vena cava, Systemic capillaries, Lungs, Pulmonary Artery, Dorsal Aorta, Posterior Vena Cava, Blood to intestines, liver, kidneys, legs, and other systemic tissues, Pulmonary circulation

Pulmonary and Systemic Circulation

Systemic Circulation

Systemic circulation is the circulation of blood throughout the body, except the heart and lungs. In systemic circulation, blood passes through the kidneys and is known as renal circulation. The kidneys filter waste from blood and then the blood passes through the small intestine and this circulation is called portal circulation. In portal circulation, the portal vein collects blood from the small intestine. The portal vein passes through the liver, which further filters the blood, extracts sugars, and stores them for later use.

Coronary Circulation

Coronary circulation is the circulation of blood through the heart. The blood vessels that carry oxygen-rich blood to the heart are called coronary arteries whereas the blood vessels that remove oxygen-less blood from the heart are called cardiac veins. For proper functioning, the heart should receive a steady supply of blood.

Main Functions

The circulatory system is responsible for the transportation of oxygen throughout the body. It also one of the means through which nutrients, water, and other chemicals are supplied to each cell of the body. Various hormones secreted by various glands are carried all over the body with the help of blood circulation. The system is also responsible for removing carbon dioxide and other waste products.

A Healthy Circulatory System

Maintaining a healthy circulatory system is important because the system distributes nutrients and oxygen to the whole body. People should eat plenty of fruits and vegetables rich in iron and antioxidants to help increase red blood cells. People should also stay away from foods rich in fat because fat can clog arteries. Large amounts of fatty foods cause weight gain. To strengthen the heart, people should exercise regularly. Jogging, swimming, and cycling are some of the fun exercises that can make the heart stronger.

SIDEBAR: DID YOU KNOW?

- The technical name for a blood pressure cuff is *sphygmomanometer*.
- Blood vessels are thousands of miles long and if strewn together, they would circle the globe two and a half times.

IMMUNE SYSTEM

The human body is prone to attacks by microorganisms such as bacteria, viruses, parasites, and so on. The immune system defends and protects the body against these foreign intruders. The immune system is made up of specialized cells, also called immune cells, and tissues that kill the disease causing germs. It works round the clock in many different ways to protect the body.

Parts of the Immune System

The cells that are involved in fighting off disease causing microorganisms are leukocytes. The leukocytes are of two types, which

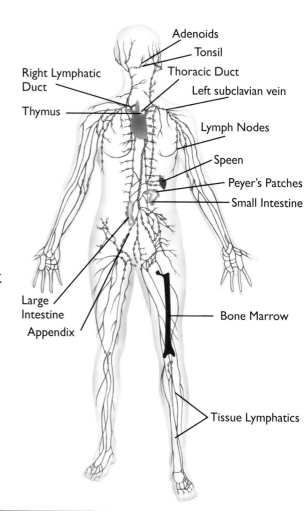

Adenoids
Tonsil
Right Lymphatic Duct
Thoracic Duct
Left subclavian vein
Thymus
Lymph Nodes
Speen
Peyer's Patches
Small Intestine
Large Intestine
Appendix
Bone Marrow
Tissue Lymphatics

WORDS TO UNDERSTAND

antigen: a substance that provokes an immune response.

leukocytes: white blood cells.

microorganisms: the organisms that cannot be seen by naked eye and are capable of causing infection in human body.

parasites: organisms that depend on other organisms for survival.

combine to seek and destroy harmful microorganisms. They circulate throughout the body through blood vessels and lymphatic vessels. Organs such as the spleen, bone marrow, and the thymus produce and store leukocytes. There are two types of leukocytes - phagocytes and lymphocytes.

Phagocytes and Lymphocytes

Phagocytes eat bacteria, viruses, and dead or injured body cells. There are three types of phagocytes - granulocytes, macrophages, and dendritic cells. The granulocytes first attack any foreign intruder in large numbers and eat them until they die. The pus that comes from infected wounds contains dead granulocytes. The macrophages and dendritic cells also feed on invaders and help in activating the rest of the immune system. On the other hand, lymphocytes remember and recognize the foreign bodies and help in destroying them. T cells and B cells are two types of lymphocytes.

How It Works

The immune system starts to work as soon as an antigen reaches the surface of the

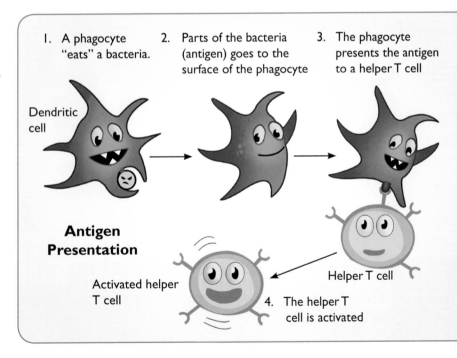

1. A phagocyte "eats" a bacteria.
2. Parts of the bacteria (antigen) goes to the surface of the phagocyte
3. The phagocyte presents the antigen to a helper T cell

Dendritic cell

Antigen Presentation

Activated helper T cell

Helper T cell

4. The helper T cell is activated

body. The external defense mechanisms of the body, including the skin and nasal hair present in the respiratory tract, get rid of the antigen by simply coughing and sneezing. However, if the antigen manages to enter the body, several types of immune cells are activated.

How Do You Know It's Working?

A person can know his immune system is working if he regains health after falling ill, if the body does not catch the same disease again, or and if cuts and wounds heal without becoming infected. Swelling and soreness around a wound may be uncomfortable but it actually indicates that the immune system is working. However, sometimes the immune system may begin to attack the body's own cells or cause an immune response to something that is not a threat. For example, allergies are caused by an overreaction of the immune system.

Boosting the Immune System

A weak immune system makes the body vulnerable to various infections and diseases. The body becomes susceptible to those diseases that it could have easily fought off. People should consume fish, cod liver oil, and garlic to make the immune system stronger. Citrus fruits, strawberries, and leafy vegetables should be included in the diet. Getting exercise regularly helps in keeping the immune system healthy.

 SIDEBAR: DID YOU KNOW?

- A lack of sleep can suppress the immune system.
- The Ancient Greek physician Hippocrates thought that illness was caused by an imbalance of the four "humors": black bile, yellow bile, blood, and phlegm.

BODY DEFENSES

This system deals with the external defense that includes physical and chemical barriers. These barriers are always ready to fight against infection and disease-causing microorganisms. Skin, mucous membranes, cilia, tears, saliva, stomach acids, and blood clotting make up the first line of defense.

Mucous Membranes

Mucous membranes in the nasal cavity and in the rest of the respiratory tract help in trapping dirt, dust, as well as microbes. The dirt, dust, and microbes trapped by the mucous membrane are removed from the respiratory tract with the help of cilia. Cilia are tiny hair on cells that line the respiratory tract. The inner lining of the large intestine produces mucus to trap foreign invaders.

Friendly Bacteria

Friendly bacteria present in stomach and intestines help in digestion as well as killing harmful bacteria and other microorganisms. Some bacteria such as lactobacillus are found in foods such as yogurt. They help the stomach in the production of stomach acids and destroy yeasts. Some bacteria ease out the digestion process by reducing any intestinal discomfort.

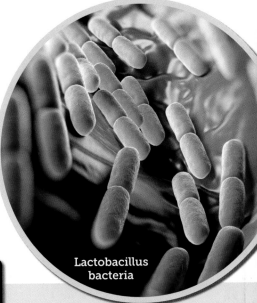

Lactobacillus bacteria

WORDS TO UNDERSTAND

antibacterial: a substance that kills or slows the growth of bacteria.

probiotic: describes something that stimulates the growth of microorganisms like bacteria.

salmonella: a rod-shaped bacteria that causes foodborne illness.

Stomach Acids

The stomach produces various enzymes and digestive juices to digest food further. These stomach acids destroy and kill harmful microorganisms, which may have been consumed while eating. The stomach acids protect the body against food poisoning caused by salmonella and other harmful bacteria.

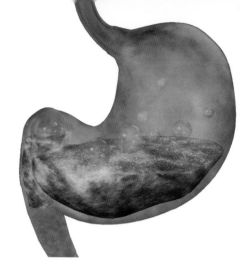

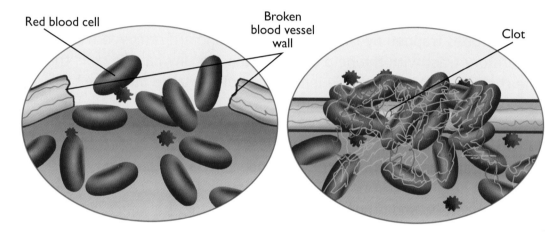

Red blood cell

Broken blood vessel wall

Clot

Blood Clotting

Microorganisms can enter inside the body when there is a cut or a bleeding wound. To restrict the entry of these microorganisms, blood cells called platelets stick together at the cut and form a clot. Blood clots are formed when blood hardens from a liquid to a solid form. As the wound begins to heal, a scab forms. A scab is the dry and hard protective cover that forms over a cut or wound during healing.

Tears, Sweat, and Saliva

If dust or anything is stuck inside the eye, tears are produced to get rid of that material. Tears prevent the eyes from infections as they contain lysozyme, an antibacterial and antiviral agent. Sweat secreted by sweat glands contains lactic acid, fatty acids, and lysozyme, which makes the skin acidic. This prevents microorganisms from growing on the skin. Saliva also contains lysozyme. The saliva mixes with the food and prevents harmful microbes from going inside the body.

Watch a video about the different types of tears.

SIDEBAR: DID YOU KNOW?

- Tears clean our eyes every time we blink.
- Probiotics are microorganisms similar to those found in the stomach and intestines.

LYMPHATIC SYSTEM

The lymphatic system is a network of organs, nodes, vessels, and ducts that produce and transport lymph throughout the body. The lymphatic organs filter out waste products from the lymph, which is then transported from tissues to the bloodstream. It is one of the parts of the immune as well as circulatory systems.

Origin of Lymph

Blood flowing in arteries is oxygenated and nutrient- and hormone rich. From arteries, blood flows into arterioles and then into tissues and lastly to into cells. Blood is now called interstitial fluid and it delivers nourishment to cells. Then it leaves cells while removing waste products. Now 90 percent of this fluid returns to the

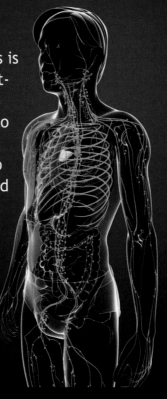
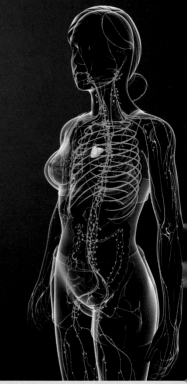

 WORDS TO UNDERSTAND

debris: waste products.

lymph: a fluid containing white blood cells.

subclavian vein: one of the two large veins on either side of the body.

heart via veins as venous blood and the remaining 10 percent is called lymph. Lymph is a clear or yellowish liquid, full of waste products and white blood cells.

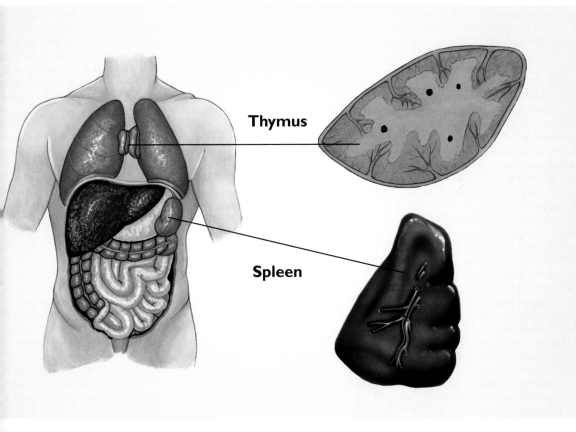

Thymus

Spleen

Lymph Organs

Bone marrow, the thymus, spleen, and lymph nodes are some of the lymph organs. Lymphocytes are produced in bone marrow and the thymus. T-lymphocytes (T cells) are produced in the thymus whereas B-lymphocytes (B cells) are produced in the bone marrow. Leukocytes and monocytes are also produced in the bone marrow. On the other hands, lymph nodes are clusters of concentrated lymphocytes and macrophages as well as lymphatic veins. The spleen is also one of the important organs of the lymphatic system. It is a reservoir of blood and purifies the blood or lymph that flows through it.

Lymph Nodes

Lymph nodes are soft, small and round organs located in clusters throughout the body. The neck, armpits, near the center of the chest, abdomen, and the groin are some of the locations where lymph nodes are easily found. Lymph nodes play a vital role in the immune system as they produce immune cells to fight off infections. They also filter lymph and remove waste products before it goes back into the circulatory system. Lymph nodes can increase or decrease in size throughout life. However, damaged nodes do not heal or regenerate.

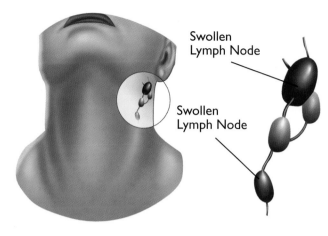

Swollen Lymph Node

Swollen Lymph Node

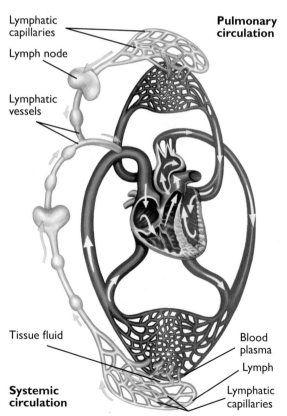

Lymphatic capillaries

Lymph node

Lymphatic vessels

Pulmonary circulation

Tissue fluid

Systemic circulation

Blood plasma

Lymph

Lymphatic capillaries

Lymph Vessels

Lymph vessels, or ducts, transport fats, proteins, and other substances in the form of lymph. These vessels are only single-cell thick and are known as lymphatic capillaries. The larger vessels are located near major veins; like veins, they have valves that allow lymph to move in only one direction.

Lymphatic Circulation

Lymph flows throughout the body along its own system of vessels. However, the system does not have a heart to pump lymph all over the body. It always flows upwards towards the neck with the help of the motions of muscles and joints. After reaching the neck, lymph mixes with the venous blood through the subclavian veins, located on sides of the neck near the collarbones. As lymph moves upwards, it passes through lymph nodes where it is filtered. Debris and pathogens are removed by the lymph nodes. The purified lymph continues its journey and after reaching the base of the neck, it flows into the subclavian veins present on either side of the neck.

SIDEBAR: DID YOU KNOW?

- **There are about 400 to 500 lymph nodes in the human body.**
- **Lymph nodes are not present in the feet.**

INTEGUMENTARY SYSTEM

Skin is the largest and most flexible organ in the body. It acts as a barrier between the body and external agents. It protects the internal organs from physical damage, microorganisms, dehydration, and helps with temperature regulation. The hard covering of skin makes it harder for disease-causing microorganisms to enter. Hairs, nails, sweat glands, and oil glands are also a part of the skin. Together they make up the integumentary system.

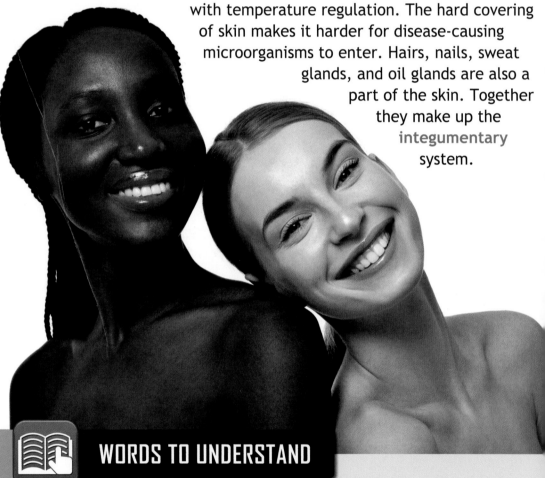

WORDS TO UNDERSTAND

basal cells: cells that are present at the lowest part of the epidermis.

excrete: to get rid of waste from the body.

integumentary: relating to an outer protective layer, such as the skin.

Parts of the Integumentary System

- **Nails** are protective coverings on the upper surface of the fingers and toes. They are formed from dead cells, which contain keratin, a fibrous protein.

- **Hair** is the threadlike growth found almost everywhere on the body. It covers and protects the body against infections and injuries. Hair also keeps the body warm by preserving heat.

- **Oil glands** present inside the skin make the skin soft and waxy. They protects the skin from chemicals and microorganisms. Sweat glands also excrete the waste out of the body and keep it healthy.

Layers of Skin

The epidermis is the outermost layer of the skin. It is very tough and protective. This layer is made up of millions of cells that are constantly dying and being replaced. The epidermis contains three main types of cells—melanocytes, keratinocytes, and langerhans.

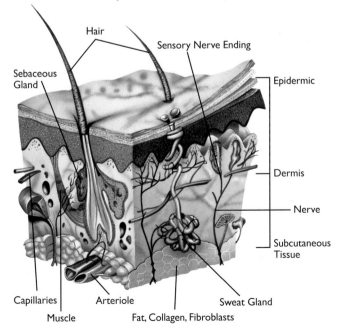

The layer of skin present below the epidermis is the dermis. This layer is made up of blood vessels, capillaries, lymph nodes, oil glands, sweat glands, and connective tissues. Oil producing sebaceous glands are also present in this layer. They surround and empty in hair follicles, lubricate the skin, and prevent it from drying out.

Subcutaneous tissue forms the innermost layer of the skin and is made up of cells that store fat. It helps the body to stay warm and regulate body temperature. The last layer of the skin also acts as a shock absorber and bears the pressure when a person falls down suddenly or receives a blow. It connects the skin to all the other tissues present beneath it.

Functions of Skin

The skin acts as a physical barrier between the body and the outside world. It has millions of nerve endings that aid in sensory reception so that the body can feel pain, touch, vibration, pressure, warmth, and coolness. It acts as a temperature regulator of the body. Sweat produced by the sweat glands evaporates and cools down the body. Blood vessels present in the skin dilate and direct blood flow towards the skin. It traps sunlight and helps in the production of vitamin D. It also helps in healing wounds as when the skin has a minor cut or abrasion; basal cells of the epidermis break away from the membrane and move around as a sheet towards the wound. When the sides of the wound meet the skin, growth stops and it returns to normal.

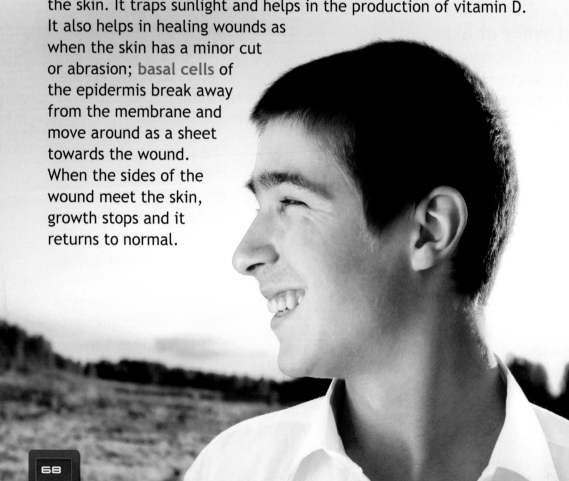

 Watch a video about skin and how it heals.

 SIDEBAR: DID YOU KNOW?

- Certain parts of the body, such as the scalp, have more follicles and therefore more hair. The soles of the feet, lips, and palms do not have hair follicles and therefore grow no hair.

- Skin has between two and five million sweat glands.

FASCINATING FACTS ABOUT BODY SYSTEMS

Respiratory System
• An average human being inhales and exhales air about 22,000 times a day.
• People can hold their breath for between 30 and 60 seconds on average. But trained divers can hold theirs a lot longer. The world record is 22 minutes!
• Oxygen depletion affects the brain because it requires 25 percent of all the oxygen the body takes in. Less oxygen affects concentration power and memory.
• Your lungs have a large amount of surface area in order to catch as much oxygen as possible. A human adult has about 300 million bronchi. If you flattened them out then they would be large enough to cover a tennis court.

Nervous System
• There are about the same number nerve cells in the human brain as there are stars in the Milky Way.
• When you learn new things, it changes the structure of your brain.
• Involuntary muscle movements are not processed by the brain.
• At birth, we can make the sounds of every language; as we learn to speak a particular language, we lose this ability.

WORDS TO UNDERSTAND

antiseptic: a substance used for cleaning wounds to keep away infections.
depletion: to reduce the amount of something.

Circulatory System

• An adult's heart beats about 42 million times a year.
• A drop of blood contains around 5 million red blood cells.
• A person has so many blood vessels that if they were laid out in a line, they'd wrap around the earth about 2.5 times.
• The bigger the body, the slower the heart rate. For example, the heart of a blue whale only beats about five times per minute.

Digestive System

• The average American eats nearly one ton of food each year.
• The esophagus is approximately 10 inches (25 cm) long. Food moves down the esophagus with the help of the contraction of muscles. This is why food will reach the stomach even if a person is sitting or lying down.
• More than 5,800 different species and strains of bacteria live inside the colon. Some of them provide nutrients like vitamin K while some fight off harmful bacteria.
• The average person makes the equivalent of two soda cans of saliva every day.

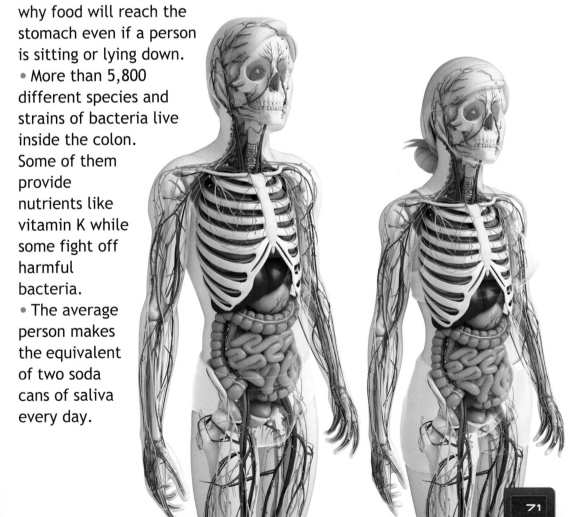

Urinary System

- Each kidney has about one million nephrons.
- Urinary tract infections are caused by bacteria in the urinary tract. They are more common in women but men can get them also.
- About 75,000 Americans are diagnosed with bladder cancer every year.
- In ancient times, people used urine as an antiseptic agent for cleaning clothes and treating wounds.

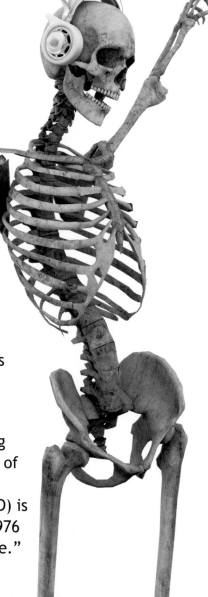

Skeletal System

- More than half the bones in the human body are in the hands and feet.
- Most people have 24 ribs but some people have an extra at the base of the neck, called a cervical rib.
- The hyoid is a bone in the neck that's shaped like a horseshoe. It's the only bone in the body that is not connected to any other bone.
- Ancient Egyptians made artificial big toes for people who had lost their own toes.

Immune System

- Sneezing, coughing, itching, and vomiting are a few of the body's ways of getting rid of harmful microorganisms.
- Severe combined immunodeficiency (SCID) is nicknamed "bubble boy disease" after a 1976 movie called "The Boy in the Plastic Bubble."

- In ancient Athens, doctors understood that people who had survived the plague would never catch the plague again, but they weren't sure why.
- Lack of sleep can impair your immune system. It may even make vaccines less effective.

Muscular System

- The human body has 650 muscles.
- An hour of reading involves about 10,000 eye movements.
- The gluteus maximus is the largest muscle in the body. It is found in the hips.
- The tongue is made up of 8 muscles.

Endocrine System

- The field of endocrinology was founded in the 1800s, but, in fact, Chinese healers had been studying the endocrine system since around 200 BC.
- Diabetes was first diagnosed by the Ancient Greek physician Hippocrates. He made the diagnosis by tasting the urine of his patients.
- The word *hormone* was coined in a study published in 1902.
- Plants do not have an endocrine system at all, but they secrete hormones anyway.

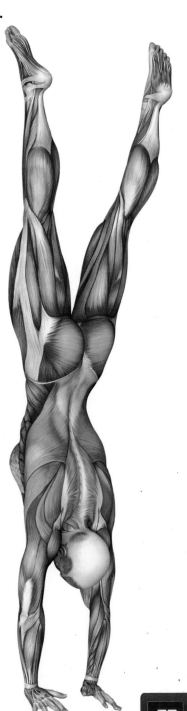

1. What is the heaviest organ?

2. Where is the pharynx and what is its function?

3. What is peristalsis?

4. What is the role of enzymes in digestion?

5. What causes goosebumps to appear?

6. How does aging affect the urinary system?

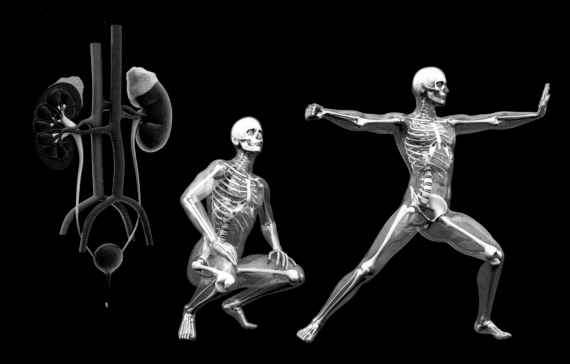

7. What is the axial skeleton?

8. Name three voluntary and three involuntary movements.

9. What are arteries?

10. What are the components of the immune system?

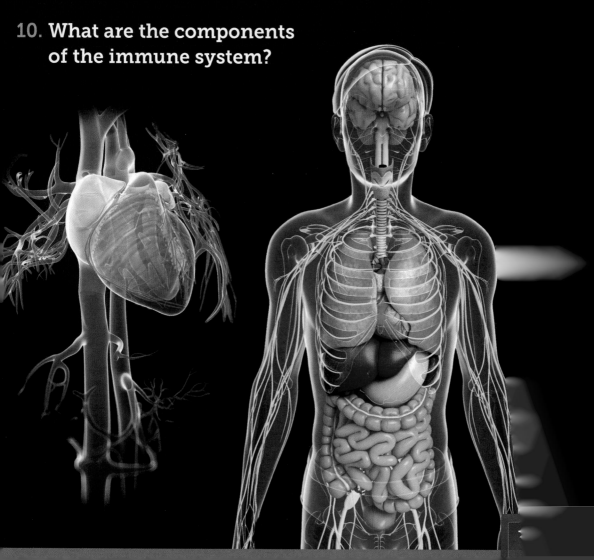

RESEARCH PROJECTS

1. Select a body system from this book and find out more about it. What are the major things that can go wrong, and what can medicine do to address those problems?

2. Using this text and other sources, find out more about Hippocrates. What did he get right about how the human body works, and what did he get wrong?

3. Print out some unlabeled diagrams of the human body and label different body systems. For example, label one copy "The Nervous System" and label the various components, and then do the same for "The Digestive System, "The Endocrine System", and so on.

4. Research the history of organ transplantation. Find out when the first transplants of major organs occurred (for example, kidney, liver, lung, heart, and so on). Turn your research into a timeline.

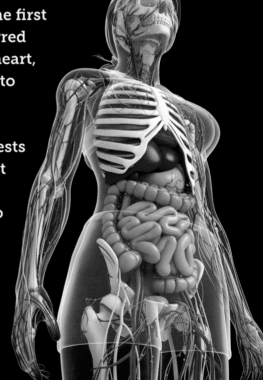

5. Select a body system that interests you, and find out more about what people can do to improve theirs. Create a list of tips and turn it into a pamphlet or poster.

FURTHER READING

Amsel, Sheri. *The Everything Kids' Human Body Book: All You Need to Know About Your Body Systems from Head to Toe!* Avon, MA: Adams Media/Simon & Schuster, 2012.

Bennett, Howard. *Fantastic Body: What Makes It Tick & How You Get Sick.* Emmaus, PA: Rodale, 2017.

Kenney, Karen. *The Circulatory System.* Minneapolis, MN: Jump!, Inc, 2017.

Weird But True Human Body. National Geographic Kids: Washington, DC, 2017.

INTERNET RESOURCES

BBC Science: Human Body & Mind
http://www.bbc.co.uk/science/humanbody/
A thorough site about human anatomy, including online games where you can test your knowledge of organs and body systems.

Teen Health and Wellness
http://www.teenhealthandwellness.com/
A comprehensive site with tons of information about the body and health.

TeensHealth: Body Basics
http://kidshealth.org/en/teens/body-basics.html
A thorough overview of the human body, including key organs and systems.

Picture Credits:

INDEX

INDEX